Poetry Two

Another
Tapestry
Of Words

Rona V Flynn

Thank you with all my heart
to those special friends
who have been such an
encouragement to me
in my writing venture x

Another Tapestry Of Words

Rona V Flynn

Index

Hello!

Like a Plate of Chips

Poetry's for sharing,
like a plate of chips.
Every one is different
and sometimes there are dips.

Poetry's for sharing,
like ice cream in the sun.
Piled high with lots of sprinkles
or dainty, and soon gone.

Poetry's for sharing,
like a good red wine,
poured slowly and enjoyed at ease.
Unhurried…given time.

Poetry's for sharing,
like a sweet bouquet.
Each flower has a different scent
to bring into your day.

Poetry's for sharing,
like a bag of chews.
Caramel or lemon fizz.
Which one will you choose?

Rona V Flynn

A Glass of Red

Where's the fun
in a glass of red
if you're drinking by yourself?
It tastes so *blah!*
It's best to leave
the bottle on the shelf.

Now a glass of wine
can bring much joy
with friends and tasty fare.
It's mellow, smooth
and goes down well.
There's nothing to compare.

When next you take
the corkscrew
and a bottle of fine red,
ensure good friends
are close at hand
with food and garlic bread.

Rona V Flynn

A Walk in the Lakes

Flowers grow on patchwork walls
along the wetted stones.
Moss and lichen spread between
with green and blue-grey tones.

Unplanned pathway leads me upward,
trudging through the flow.
Clambering to reach the hilltop,
hoping soon the rain will slow.

Swathes and shades of browns and greens
flow over rise and fall.
Windswept trees grow random scattered
on the craggy cliff top wall.

Dark and cold, the rippled waters
mirror well the cloudy sky.
Then steep meanders lead me through the dale
where I see kestrels fly.

At last, all effort full rewarded ~
To the summit wild and free.
Across the hills I look in wonder
drinking in all I can see.

Can my spirit soar much higher
in this pleasant holy place?
At one with hills and sky and nature ~
Rapt in Earth's profound embrace.

And yet, I see celestial colours
bowed within the brightening blue.
Bejewelled droplets dance in sunlight,
painting sky with heaven's dew.

This is nature…

Rona V Flynn

Hills and streams,
Mountains and lakes.
Wild flowers.
What could be better…

When I listen in the still of the evening,
I'm reminded that I'm just a small part of
something so much greater.

Blackbird

Year on year you are ever here,
perched nobly on the highest place.
Sing your heavenly refrain.
Yellow beak sharp against the sky,
bright before the darkening blue.
Black eyes echo starlight
cloaked in ebony velvet ~
dark, timeless, without ending.

As red wine to the lips
is your song to my heart.
Rich and deep.

You call to all you see
I am singing, listen to me.
Hear my song and know I am here.
Each note, crystal clear perfection,
piercing cool unhurried air.
Gently, you whisper a soft melody,
then bursting forth, you pour from within
the fullness and depth of your potent tones.

I close my eyes and drink.
My cup is full.
My soul sated.

Rona V Flynn

Tarr Steps Ancient Clapper Bridge in Exmoor.
Doesn't it look just like a spine!

This bridge is over three thousand years old.

Earth's Bones

Earth's bones are rock and stones,
created from dust and matter and breath,
baked and moulded in the depths.

Earth's frame is fashioned by flame
way down deep in searing heat ~
where minerals, gas and magma meet.

Precious stones lie in the bones.
Rubies, sapphires, amethysts,
crushed and pressed and rainbow-kissed.

Earth's bones creak and groan,
shifting slow as they crack and burn ~
Holding fast as we slowly turn.

And here we stand upon this land ~
upon the dirt that holds new birth
and clothes the bones of planet Earth.

Rona V Flynn

Catherine's Ruins (Lydiate Abbey)

Ruins of her sacred place.
Of mason's pride in stony lace.
Of sunshine through the rosy hue
of stained glass in this holy space.

Ancient days and ways to be,
in life's forgotten history
of candles, charms and chanted psalms,
and wretched prayers on bended knee.

For centuries, bereft she's stood,
her chiselled stone and polished wood
diminished by the passing time.
A testament from times once good.

Grass grows around the ancient walls
but empty bell tower yet stands tall.
It reaches high against the sky,
above the open sandstone hall.

While sunset paints the sacred stone
a blackbird sings his psalms alone,
and summer breeze sways whispering trees
in prayerful chants and priestly tones.

So life thrives still, within this place,
and song and colour fill the space
where once so long ago a throng
joined voices to say prayers and grace.

Rona V Flynn

Affectionately known as Lydiate Abbey,
the remains of St Catherine's Chapel lie in the village
of Lydiate, Lancashire.

The chapel was originally built by the
Ireland family during the late 1400's and
records reveal the secret burial of priests after the
English Reformation.

When something is created just for you,
embrace its preciousness.

Gift

Perfect imperfection.
Home-crafted just for you.
Created by a giving heart,
a seed of thought that grew.

Though rough around the edges,
each part holds depth and time,
filled with ponderings and musings
and uniquely formed design.

Given with an open heart,
to be received in kind,
A precious gift imparted
will uplift the heart and mind.

Appreciating sentiment
is power to the soul.
To see the weight behind it
is to see it as a whole.

Rona V Flynn

I discovered this poem in a ragged old envelope
from times long gone.
My son was two, or maybe just three years old
when I wrote it.
When he was born, I truly *was*
overwhelmed with love.

Peek-a-boo!

Firstborn

A mischievous smile is my child.
Tears from large sorrowful eyes.
Unstoppable, yet gentle.
Laughter is my child,
like fast-flowing water over pebbles and stones.
Curiosity, wide-eyed wonder and triumph is he.
Adventurous and hungry for knowledge.
But most of all he is love.
He loves life and everything in it,
untainted yet by a cruel world.
He is innocent and hateless,
filled with endless love and trust.
Perfect.
I have never been more filled.

Rona V Flynn 1974

Not fog exactly,
but a beautiful misty morning
at Derwent Water, Keswick.

Fog

I've got my own white blanket,
a place where I can hide.
The world is so much smaller
when I'm tucked up safe inside.
It covers all, and I can stay
wrapped up until it's passed.
Too often it will fade away
when I wish it would last.

Rona V Flynn Nov' 1976

It's rarely foggy these days
but I still like it.
(Unless I'm driving).
Do you love it or hate it?

21

Four Faces

Smouldering explosive power.
Bringer of long day and hour.
Turns her face on us and smiles,
draws us nearer for a while.

Then, her eyes begin to close
as flimsy layers of feathered rose
drift across the vibrant Bright,
and day makes room for longer night.

Cloaked in white unearthly veil,
silvery, and cold and pale.
Paper circle small and bare,
withdrawn and silent in the air.

Pastel yellow melts away
the icy shroud. It warms the day
and reaches down to touch the earth,
to scatter life and spread new birth.

Four faces of our solar star,
each shine their light in turn on our
defenceless world to make it live ~
and we receive that which they give.

Rona V Flynn

Jingling bells.

One of my absolute favourites.

I Like the Sound of

I like the sound of children playing in the park.
Laughter, screams and cries of fun
soar across the sky.
Lapping waves, washing over gritty ancient sand.
Thunder rolling through the clouds ~
a sound I can't deny.

I like the sound as raindrops tap on my umbrella.
A gust of wind through summer trees ~
rustling delight.
Jingling bells, they make me smile
wherever they may ring.
A blackbird from the treetop
brings me joy before the night.

I like the sound of laughter, wherever it may be.
The tinkling of clear crystal,
resounding through the air.
The crunching of fresh-fallen snow,
white and crisp and new.
The minor key ~
it touches me in ways that lay me bare.

Rona V Flynn

Remembering Liberté Square,
Saint-Guilhem-Le-Desert.

Phew! It was hot!

Melting in The Shade

We sit against the high wall ~
our refuge in the shade.
Fanning our red faces
and sipping lemonade.

Roasted by the fierce sun
and gasping for fresh air,
we fade and wilt in searing heat.
I squint across the glare.

The parasols are frozen
for want of summer breeze
to move the air about them
and bring a little ease.

A fountain looks inviting
in the centre of the square,
but we lack the crucial wherewithal
to move from here to there.

This sun, it has *no* mercy.
It pours with all its might
a heat that leaves us begging
for the warm air of the night.

Rona V Flynn

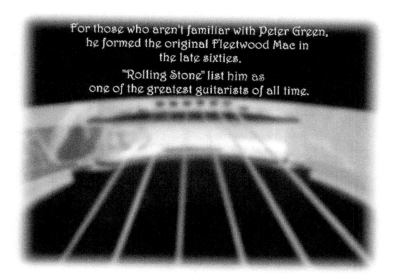

For those who aren't familiar with Peter Green, he formed the original Fleetwood Mac in the late sixties.

"Rolling Stone" list him as one of the greatest guitarists of all time.

Peter Green's Blues

When he sings and plays
he speaks volumes from the depths.
Scooping down into my boots
with riffs that catch my breath.

He carries me on every note,
stretching out my soul
and bathing me in honey,
dripping smooth and slow.

He soothes me deep. He stirs me
with exquisite, mellow tone.
That moment, he takes everything
I have, or ever owned.

His soul creates the richest sounds,
sweet and blue and long.
He leaves me feeling good inside
and I can hear his song.

Rona V Flynn

Wherewithal

When you haven't got the wherewithal
to do the things you like.
When your get up and go has got up and gone
and your oomph has taken flight.

When your energy's down to two percent
and it's just not worth the try.
When you know you'll never make it,
so you let it pass you by.

Relax, embrace the hour and rest.
Doze a while and snore.
Indulge yourself and let it be.
The need, is to restore.

Rona V Flynn

If Only

She watched him out the corner
of her eye across the way.
Monday, Wednesday, Friday
in *The Happy Place Café.*

Four weeks on, they'd pass and nod
and maybe even smile.
He'd get his black coffee
and she'd get camomile.

An hour spent so near, yet far ~
Almost too much to bear.
The briefest glance would flip her heart
through raptures and despair.

For two weeks he'd been missing.
She stared into her cup
and pondered on the chances of him
ever showing up.

The waitress said *I wonder where
the man across has gone?*
For she had watched them closely
from the bench she leaned upon.

Then in he came dishevelled,
with a mess of auburn hair.
He ordered his black coffee
and a very large éclair.

When she glanced towards him,
their eyes met and they blushed.
It felt so good to see his smile
which she returned, quite flushed.

The waitress brought his coffee
and winked as she passed by.
She longed to say *hello* to him
and cleared her throat to try.

Then the blonde burst through the door,
all glamourous and chic.
'There you are!' She said with flair,
and kissed him on the cheek.

Stunned, she took a gasp of breath
and made a silent groan.
Whatever was I thinking!
I really should have known.

When they left, she noticed
that the woman glanced her way.
Although she didn't say a word
He's mine! She heard her say.

He and the vivacious blonde
flopped onto his settee.
'I'll put the kettle on.' She said.
'Let's have a cup of tea.

*Ninety-four was a good age
and she was pretty strong.'*
"Yes, she was amazing
and I'm glad her life was long.

There wasn't much to go through
as she kept a tidy space.
Just some books and photographs
of our old summer place."

*'I meant to tell you yesterday,
I've snaps of you and me.
Just after we moved to the coast ~
I think when we were three.*

I liked her by the way.' She said.
'I thought she seemed quite nice.
But next time, sit right next to her,
that would be my advice.'

"*Oo!*" He said and cringed a bit.
"We'll have to wait and see.
I'm glad to know you like her though,
she seems just right for me."

'I'll be gone tomorrow,
my plane leaves half past two.
Tell me how it goes with her,
I want to hear from you.'

She found a cosy corner
at *The New Place* in the square.
How could I have been such a fool
to think that he might care!

He looked once more across the cafe
and to the empty pew.
How could I have been such a fool
to think she liked me too!

Rona V Flynn

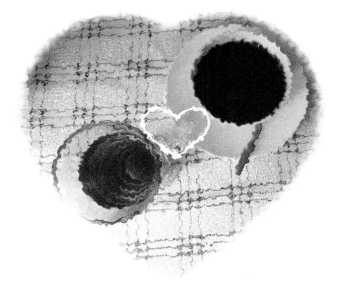

Oh! What might have been...

Givers and Takers

There are all kinds of people in this world,
with all kinds of need and want.
Some souls are never satisfied
while some remain content.

Those whose hearts are *giving*
are never bound by greed.
They take each day with what it brings.
They have what they will need.

They do not want the trappings
of a world with much to give.
They're easy to spend time with
and quick to live, let live.

Mean spirited will *take* and *take*
and never feel at peace.
Their needs are never satisfied.
Their *wants* will never cease.

They crave what they know is not theirs,
they 'own' what's not to own,
to fill a need inside themselves
that's rooted to the bone.

Their stony hearts are as hard as flint,
they act with power and might.
While stepping over kindly souls
they *take* it as their right.

Some have soft and tender hearts
that hurt and scar and bleed.
They give when takers *take* from them
to satisfy their need.

One day we will consider
the life that we have led.
What was, and things that might have been ~
The things we may have said.

Though it may be impossible
to change what's past and gone,
we still can live *today* with *give,*
before our days are done.

Rona V Flynn

To smile is good for us.

Kindness

Be a little giving
as you go about your day.
Share a smile once in a while
to help folk on their way.

Show a little tenderness
when they pass you by.
Seek to share some warmth and care
and look them in the eye.

Notice the unnoticed.
Give a little space.
Think outside your own divide.
Create a kindly place.

Rona V Flynn

A man, his dog, and nature

Rapeseed

Endless seas of yellow,
acid sharp and bright.
Tossing gently in the fields
of blinding dayglo light.

They pierce my eyes like laser.
Engraving on my brain
images of beauty paired with
penetrating pain.

Breakers roll towards me.
Then, bidding their farewell,
they flood across the hillside
weaving patterns through the swell.

Rona V Flynn

The Scotch Piper is the oldest pub in Lancashire, UK
and dates as far back as the 1200's.
It was initially named The Royal Oak.
Sections of the original Oak tree, round which
the pub was built, are still visible in
the Tap Room.
If you look carefully, you can make out the large
wooden barrel in front of the door.

Drayman

He heaves the barrels to and fro
from one cold cellar to the next,
downing his pint before moving on.
One last time, he climbs aboard,
squinting in afternoon sun.

Street lamps light his way back home,
fleshy fists hammer hard.
The door is finally opened.
Staggering through, he crashes to the floor.
His pockets are empty.

Rona V Flynn

It was comical to watch
these two ducks and their moorhen friend
sliding about on the frozen canal last winter.
They didn't seem to mind cold
feet at all, but the ice was beginning to melt.

Blue

There is a pain.
It sits in wait.
Before we realise too late the wound is struck.
The hurt is raw.
The heart defenceless, bare and sore.

There is a pain.
The twisting blade
brings with it such a sombre shade.
It reaches to the hidden place
and ministers a cold embrace.

There is a pain.
From way down deep
it swells ~ awakened from its sleep.
Then heaving currents pull us through
to all-consuming darkest blue.

Rona V Flynn

How boring life would be
without *Difference*.

Sometimes

Sometimes… you might just think
your thoughts are a little bit dippy…
Way outside the proverbial box
and maybe a little bit *Hippy*.

Sometimes… you might decide
you're just a little bit random…
Strolling along your own sweet way
and a little bit out of tandem.

But don't forget that, just like you,
we're all a little bit different too.
For no two humans are the same
and we're *all* just a little bit *iffy*…

Rona V Flynn

Secrets

A secret shared can soon find wings
and wend its way through tongues that sing.
Sneaking round behind closed doors,
in furtive whispers sharing more.
Feeding as it drips and sows.
Bleeding as it twists and flows.
Breaking hearts and peace of mind ~
Breaking trust is so unkind.
If someone shares their soul with you
be sure to keep their secret true.

Rona V Flynn

The Flood That Roared

Standing alone, her scream whispered
Standing with many, their whispers screamed
The drop of rain became a mighty deluge
The mighty deluge became a flood
The flood that roared

Rona V Flynn

Me Too

When many become one,
they will be heard.

Little Sparrow

There was a little sparrow
who would meet me near the gate.
He'd follow me along the wall,
then to my door and wait.
He'd flutter and he'd flap for me
as I turned the key.
I'll be round the back! I'd say,
and then he'd fly to see.

Sure enough, there he was
standing just outside,
Looking up expectantly,
to me stood just inside.
He'd fluff his downy feathers
and he'd flap his little wings,
Chirpy-cheeping all the time
to ask what I would bring.

He'd never come so close
as to take something from my palm,
But there he stood so near each day,
so cheery, sweet and calm.
Then, just as I walked inside,
he fluttered and he flapped
straight into my kitchen!
I thought he would be *trapped!*

How frightened he would surely be
in such a strangely place!
I felt so sure he'd harm himself
in trying to escape.
But when he saw me standing there,
he calmly flew outside
and waited by the door again
for me to sit beside.

Alas! He failed to greet me
and each day I would look out.
Little Sparrow was no more
and gone without a doubt.
I did my best to try not rest
my thoughts upon his fate,
Yet always hoped to see him there
and sometimes I would wait.

I never have forgotten
how he used to come and chat,
The daring little sparrow
who would twitter as we sat.
That little ray of sunshine
who always made my day
has left a tender memory
that will forever stay.

Rona V Flynn

Bath time

Conversation

Just like a box of chocolates,
we don't know what we'll get.
There could be frost, it may be hot,
We might get soaking wet.

We leave the house with shorts on,
our legs are freezing cold.
We wear a sweater when it's grey
but sunshine takes a hold.

It's teeming, then it's roasting.
What's happened to the flowers?
We love the sun, it makes us smile,
but now we need the showers.

The air today is humid,
just right for muggy frizz.
Tomorrow could be gale force
but that's the way it is.

At least there's conversation
when we take the chance to walk,
and the subject is the weather
when we meet someone and talk.

Rona V Flynn

The British are known for talking about the weather,
and who can blame us, it's **so** unpredictable!

Remembering

I know nothing of the pain and fright
and fear of boys who went to fight.
Of mums whose lives with sons were brief ~
Their lifelong legacies of grief.

I know nothing of dads who lost their way,
their sense of life and their sense of play.
Of anxious wives who waited for
that dreaded knock on their front door.

I know nothing of the bodies lay
beneath the feet in battle's fray.
The trenches, stenches, and the cries
of best pals killed before their eyes.

I know nothing of the pain of war,
the horror and the sights they saw.
Of watching comrades lose their mind.
Of knowing someone's left behind.

Of these things, I know nothing…

But I do know, when I woke today
I could open my door and be on my way.
The sky was clear and the streets were free ~
No checkpoints, guns or military.

I'm grateful for the peace I knew
when I was young ~ and my children too.
Though we had very little when I was small,
peace was woven through it all.

I don't understand the ways of war
and I truly wish there were no more.
But I'm grateful to those who gave for me,
So I can live a life that's free...

And to them, I say thank you.

Rona V Flynn

By the end of WW1 80,000 had been diagnosed with
shell-shock (PTSD).
Poor mental health can have a huge impact on our
lives and those close to us,
thank goodness we're beginning to talk about it.

Tick Tock - Which one are *you?*

Tick Tock

Tick, tock, ticking clock,
How long must we wait?
Watch the dial and wait a while.
Someone's always late.

Clock ticks, never quick.
Check the time again.
Seeds of doubt are sown about,
Will they turn up and when?

The world won't wait when we are late,
time will not stop its pace.
Is it fair to leave them where
there should be empty space.

Do you turn up early
or are you always late?
Is your eye kept on the time
or do you make them wait?

Rona V Flynn

Heavy Key

There lies a door inside her soul.
It's tightly locked and hard to find.
She will not turn the heavy key,
releasing that which lies behind.

There's none can reach to soothe the void
within the chasm, dark and deep.
It stays untouched, she leaves it be ~
behind the door, where it will keep.

Rona V Flynn

Robin Williams
Comedian & Actor

1951 – 2014

So sad,
A few of my favourites ~
Mork & Mindy, Awakenings, Patch Adams,
Dead Poets Society, August Rush,
Millennium Man, Good Will Hunting

Robin Williams

He had us falling in the aisles.
with wacky screwball fun.
We loved him, he was such a laugh
and talented bar none.

His face was ever changing
yet always stayed the same.
The voices were hilarious
and widespread grew his fame.

He didn't always play the clown,
he often made us weep.
Such tragedy portrayed so well,
so heart-rending and deep.

From where did he become these souls
to know how they would feel!
For we believed in every word
his tender heart revealed.

Such joy he spread about him.
What agony inside.
He slipped away to end the pain.
By daybreak he had died.

Rona V Flynn

First Love

He lifted my heart when I saw him.
His smile was warm and sweet.
The two of us were starry eyed
every time we'd meet.

I can see his face quite clearly.
His eyes were cloudless blue
with lashes that were curled and long.
His hair was wavy too.

Though many years have passed,
I do recall him now and then.
I wonder how he is
and if we'll ever meet again.

He looks out from the photograph,
sitting next to me
with his double diamond.
I had Cherry B.

So young and innocent back then
and my love felt so true.
He was the first to steal my heart
but I stole his heart too.

Rona V Flynn

How beautiful to find someone
who *sees* us and *loves* us.

I See You

Who will say *I see you*?
I see beyond your gaze.
I see your depth,
I see your truth,
I see your unseen ways.

Who will say *I see you*?
I see beneath your skin.
I see your light,
I see your dark,
I see the *you* within.

Who will say *I see you*?
I see into your soul.
I see your flaws,
I see your strengths,
I see you as a whole.

Who will say *I see you*…

Rona V Flynn

Let them be little

Let them be little a little bit more,
encourage the child in their soul.
Let them be silly with giggles and fun,
leave their wonder untainted and whole.

They have all their lives to be grown-ups
with worry and stress and such things.
Let them escape for as long as they can
all the cares adulthood will bring.

The world tries so hard to *squeeze* small into big
while they're still only little in years.
Help them to love themselves just as they are,
and give comfort through heart-break and tears.

They need to be carefree in this troubled world,
child-like and open and sweet.
Free to feel happy with life's simple ways
before innocence bids its retreat.

Rona V Flynn

Old Man of the Woods

Old man of the woods, roots deep and stood
a thousand years and more.
Though mighty winds may test your strength,
you endlessly endure.

Tell me Old Man, what is it you see
when years long slow unfold.
Kings and minstrels, Knights and duels,
battlefields of old?

> "Roots fixed deep in history
> I've stood here this long age.
> I watch the world its circles make.
> I see the seasons change.
>
> Mistletoe decks my winter boughs
> and catkins hang in spring.
> Summer greens turn slow to reds
> when autumn spreads her wings.
>
> Many acorns have I shed
> with many yet foretold.
> A hidden feast for those who hunt
> through autumn browns and golds.

My agéd trunk is rough and grey,
deep-creviced, thick and warm.
Creatures weave within, without
where bark is ripped and torn.

Butterflies reborn take wing,
and bats by moon's pale light.
Chicks stay nestled close and warm
until their maiden flight.

I offer refuge from the rain,
Cool shade in summer sun.
Ease for weary travellers who may
sit 'til rest is done.

My heart is warmed to know and see
the seasons ebb and flow.
The circle turns without an end
and ever will be so."

Beautiful old man, wrinkled and gnarled,
of glorious renown.
Wise old man, long stood and deep
in earth's sweet fragrant ground.

I offer you my heartfelt thanks
for all you freely share.
It gladdens me to wait and know
and feel that you are there.

Rona V Flynn

What would we do without our beautiful trees...

Sepia Memories

Unexpected memories
fall from dusty cupboards
crammed full of aging snapshots
in a mind that's filled with stuff.
Like fading sepia photographs
hidden in a corner,
out of reach, forgotten
because life is full enough.

Longest summer holidays
of playing on the corner
and swinging round the lamp post.
Staying out 'til really late.
Roaring fires in winter
and ice inside the windows.
Running home through sun-showers,
and wet shoes on the grate.

Sitting on the doorstep in the
sun by wild pink roses,
breathing in the summer scents
beneath a clear blue sky.
Overgrowing grass and
uncut hedges line the pathway
leading to the currant bush,
with irises nearby.

Freezing winter mornings,
shivering while dressing.
Hot shoes from the oven
made my feet as warm as toast.
Chilblains by the fire.
Watching pretty patterns
of hot coals mesmerising
as I sit and slowly roast.

Rhubarb dipped in sugar,
mouth-wateringly sour.
The path of bricks with
upturned empty jars along the edge.
Gran's yellow bright canary
singing songs out in the sunshine.
The mangle in the wash-house and
the flowering privet hedge.

Grown-ups playing cards
and laughing loud around the table.
Toes ruffling the rag rug
by the huge imposing grate.
Black kettle on the trivet,
spouting steam and spitting.
Gran's house was a curious
and interesting place.

Street parades and funfairs
on the big field every May Day.
The jingling of Morris Dancers
ringing out their bells.
Chair-o-planes and swing-boats,
Bumper cars and waltzer.
Candyfloss and diesel
fill the air with heady smells.

Mum's lilac coat, the fragrance
of her red lipstick and make-up.
Uncle Charlie singing
as he played guitar for me.
Cousin-fun with Elwyn when
he visited each summer.
Fishing through the letter box
to reach the hidden key.

The past is like old photographs
suspended in their timeline.
Frozen 'til a smell or touch
recalls them from afar.
They tumble unexpected
to our conscious mind and catch us.
They live once more, they move us
and remind us who we are.

Rona V Flynn

What are your Sepia memories?
Let them tumble...

73

Violin

At first, I thought my eyes had glimpsed
a vision from a mislaid dream.
I looked again and caught my breath.
A violin beneath the beam!

In shabby case with threadbare cloth.
Surrounded by spent gifts and throws.
Dimly lit, almost unseen
and hanging with the worn-out clothes.

My heartstrings played a minor key
awakened by my spirit muse.
A sombre mood soft kissed the air
for violin midst ragged blues.

Mellow tones no longer heard
by spellbound souls with ears to lend.
Songs unsung and hearts unchanged.
No sweet escape where minds transcend.

Breath now still and life full bled,
a wretched sight in sad repose.
I turned to leave, but looked again
to toss a final dream-spun rose.

Rona V Flynn

Is the world getting smaller or bigger?
I can't decide.
It most definitely grows more
complicated with time.

When I Was Young

When I was young, I saw through rosy glass,
wide-eyed, naive and free.
I'd greet each day anew with hope
and trust all I could see.

When I was young, small things made me smile,
and everything was near.
I was innocent, and ignorant
of life outside my sphere.

When I was young, life was filled with less,
and choices were but few.
But through long days we always
filled our time with things to do.

Rona V Flynn

Enjoy your sleep wherever it may be ~
Perhaps a
warm siesta in the shade?

Sleep

Like a leaf on a warm millpond, I float,
suspended by the merest touch of reality.
Fading gossamer delivers me to
slow freefall through mists of no man's land.
Lost between truth and fantasy
I lie paralysed by exquisite promise.
The edge of a dream gently calls
through ethereal haze of other worlds.
At last, sweet raptures softly whisper
from the deep hollows,
the place of light and dark,
where dreams are waiting to be set free…

Rona V Flynn

When you meet up with an old friend
you haven't seen for
a very long time.

Old Friends

Like a comfy shoe re-found.
Warm, familiar, moulded round
your flesh. Worn-in and not too tight.
Holding tender parts just right.

They know your bones and tricky bits.
They rode the storms and slips and trips.
Feet back in that safe place again
where they know you and you know them.

Rona V Flynn

So many interesting shops
gone forever.

Shutters and Tumbleweed

Now it's just a ghost town
where empty streets lie dim.
Shutters, boards and locked up doors,
desolate and grim.

No buzz or joy or hubbub.
No wares to window-shop
or touch and try before we buy.
Nowhere to chat and stop.

Litter blows like tumbleweed
past shops once filled with soul.
Neglected signs, unoccupied.
The death knells sound their toll.

Shutters rattle in the wind.
In plaintiff voice they cry
No business here! Their falling tears
meet rain from stormy skies.

Though life goes on, we will lament
the joys of shopping past.
No more to see, that which has been
replaced by all things fast.

Rona V Flynn

Damsels and Dragons

Marshes and ditches, rivers and streams
hide underworld secrets
and darkest of dreams.
Lurking in shadows and hidden from sight,
lying in wait and embraced by the night.

While longer days near and waters grow warm.
While skies grow much brighter
and bring early dawn.
He watches and waits,
keeping well his disguise,
looking up through the silver and to the sunrise.

The day is now here and the time set just right.
Stepping out from the mire
he climbs up to the heights.
He heaves off his mantle and stops to take breath,
now helpless and weak since his rise from the depths.

From the darkest of nights to the longest of days,
labour complete
he now rests in the haze.
The sun weaves its gold through his delicate furls
by gently unfolding each wing from its curls.

Swift fills the air with bright colours that shine
like rich jewels made of
sunshine and moonlight entwined.
Like delicate lace spun in silver and green,
and flashes of turquoise with midnight between.

Though his beauty will dazzle his life will be brief,
but his love will lay offspring
in waters beneath.
They too will find darkness,
and biding their time they will
wait for their moment…and *their* time to shine.

Rona V Flynn

Damselflies and Dragonflies are almost fantastical
creatures.
They can spend over a year in murky waters
before emerging into the warm sunshine for the first
time.
Here they will shed their final outer layer,
free their delicate wings and ~
if they're lucky ~
flit and fly for just a few weeks
before their demise.

Not a Store Detective,
but a soldier guarding
Edinburgh Castle, Scotland.

Store Detective

'Hiding' in plain sight,
she glanced deftly down the aisle.
Handbag poised sedately
in regal queen-esque style.
Her hair was in a French pleat,
she wore a fifties coat.
Different but I liked it -
whatever floats your boat.
She followed me with stealth
and furtive browsing from nearby.
Replacing lipstick, I moved on
unsettled, I won't lie.
As I turned the corner,
second thoughts spun me around.
I'm so sorry! I laugh cheerfully
as we both rebound.
Startled only briefly,
she had nothing to say
and swiftly turned upon her heels,
to scurry on her way.
How strange. I thought,
Just two of us in this big empty shop,
why would she stay so close to me?
And then the penny dropped.

Rona V Flynn

Dandelion Clocks

Time Opens Our Eyes

Time opens our eyes
and helps us to see
that whatever we think,
It's okay being me.

Things we've been taught
and things we have heard
condition our minds
to believe every word.

Unfurling before us
they twist and they turn,
revealing the things
we've mistakenly learned.

Those tangles and hurts
we all carry inside us
begin to unravel
with time and the tide.

Rona V Flynn

Take a deep, beautiful,
sweet, clean breath

Rain

A rush of wind blows round my face.
I see the threatening skies change pace,
then the rain falls.
Sparrows shelter in the trees'
darkened shiny polished leaves.
A Magpie calls.

Pools of dancing water bond
and spill across the stones beyond
as pathways flood.
Increasing circles spin and grow
transforming sodden earth below
to miry mud.

Downpour slows its angry shout.
Green hues tint the air about
as sky brightens.
Sparkling droplets reflect depth.
My lungs are filled with pure clean breath.
Senses are heightened.

Now there is a different light.
It's cool and clear, and fresh and bright ~
invigorating.
Wet stones dry to bluish grey,
water slowly fades away,
the sun is waiting.

Rona V Flynn

In the UK, the Summer Solstice is celebrated at Stonehenge.

These ancient stones have stood in the county of Wiltshire, England for around 5,000 years.

The tallest stone measures 8.71 metres (28½ ft), 2.13 metres of which lie underground. Stonehenge is about an hour's drive from the famous festival site, Glastonbury.

Longest Day

Sacred stones rise up against
a fiery crimson dawn,
kissed by nature's hourglass.
The longest day is born.
Wakened sun floods ancient circle,
casting shadows long
as giants greet our Summer Solstice,
singing their Midsummer song.

Rona V Flynn

Until our final breath,
wherever we go, whatever we do,
we leave behind us a little of who we are.

How much will live on
when we're finally gone?

Lacy Fingers

Don't walk too near the water
when you stroll along the shore.
For there, her lacy fingers lie in wait.
They'll creep along the sand
to steal your fading footprints fast,
and capture them before it's left too late.

She takes them to the deep,
where they wander aimlessly
as they search the seas and oceans for their home.
Then, from the depths she calls them,
for when the time is right
they no longer will be called upon to roam.

Because life turns in circles
without endings or beginnings,
they'll be reunited with the only *one*.
The one whom they've been seeking,
who will make them feel complete,
and take them back into the earth where they belong.

Rona V Flynn

Mindfulness.
Body and mind.

Rhythm of Breath

Deep and luscious stillness calls.
I rest to find that space within.
Mellow softness gently falls
with every breath of out and in.

Rona V Flynn

It so good when special people
in our lives release the gold within us.

Mining for Gold

We all have gold within us
of varied depth and hue.
Hidden veins of pure delight
reflecting hidden you.

There are different routes to find it,
through different kinds of doors,
and different humans mine it
from our out and inner core.

Rooted in the darkness,
it lies ready and refined
for those who bring it to the light ~
as they will make it shine.

Rona V Flynn

Eleanor

Eleanor didn't plan to
die alone without a man
but sometimes people just don't come together.
No amount of money
can buy someone to love and
it's so hard to find someone to love forever.

There's something more about her
when she picks up her guitar,
you could swear it almost gently starts to weep.
She has so much inside her
but she hides her love away,
like the face cream in the fancy jar she keeps.

She fills her time with this and that
and sometimes takes a ride.
Her favourite is the mystery tour to date.
It goes down Penny Lane
and then on to Strawberry Fields,
up the long and winding road and to the gate.

Yesterday, tomorrow
and today are all the same.
All you need is love her friends would say.
Let it be, I feel fine. Is always her reply.
I'm happy with my lot, so come what may.

He saw her standing there,
with a ticket in her hand.
Hello, can I sit with you on the bus.
Look! Here comes the sun he cheered,
nodding to the sky.
She laughed and said, *well alright, if you must.*

His kiss tasted like honey,
then he pushed a piece of paper
in her palm, *from me to you,* and said *Goodbye.*
Golden slumbers filled her eyes,
she dreamed of love forever.
In the morning she saw diamonds in her skies.

I wanna hold your hand he said,
and then reached out with his.
She took it and they both went for some food.
I still don't know your name,
you wouldn't tell me yesterday, you just smiled.
He smiled again, and said *it's Jude.*

Rona V Flynn

And they lived Happy ever after
(in the market place)
I couldn't resist just one more song.

Our experiences
of the Christmas season
can differ so much.

Dreading Christmas

Like snow it falls.
A frenzied blizzard,
glittering and bright.
A blur of sameness.

Cutting, cold winds
rip through streets,
howling and moaning.
Chilling to the bone.

Teeming rain
beats its drum.
Raging torrents,
hot and stinging.

Steely sky. Waiting.
Horizon swept bare.
Lifeless and empty.
Barren and bleak.

Rona V Flynn

Christmas Day

Simply this…

Kith and Kin
Glass of cheer
Feeling happy
Loved ones near

Swapping gifts
Hug and kiss
Cracker jokes
Reminisce

Empty plates
Dishes done
Top up glasses
Games and fun

Christmas cake
Sweet mince pies
Lie back, feet up
Close your eyes

Rona V Flynn

The words of this poem
fit perfectly to the popular tune for
Robert Burns 'Auld Lang Syne' 1788.

For the Sake of Old Lang Syne

So swift the year has passed us by
and suddenly we're here.
Once more we will sing Auld Lang Syne
and welcome the New Year.

Again, we will look back in time
and to the future too.
We'll pause and think about our past
and all that we've come through.

For life, though such a privilege,
will always bring regrets,
but as we live each day, the years
will help us to forget.

Let's make the most of all we have,
and cherish all that's dear.
Let's live and love, then love again
and celebrate with cheer.

Rona V Flynn

Happy New Year to You!
I hope it's a good one. x

Tales

Of Wisdom

Friends

There was a man who, as he grew older, considered his life path in comparison to that of his oldest friends. He had observed how exceptionally gifted they were, each one in the different spheres they had chosen.

One friend was a Professor of great wisdom, he had published many books and regularly lectured in prestigious venues. The man often purchased recordings of his friend's lectures and had copies of all his books.

Another friend was an artist whose paintings were exhibited in some of the world's most famous galleries. A signed print of his favourite painting hung above the man's mantel and he often stood before it, appreciating the intricate detail and colour of the work.

The third friend was renowned for his exceptional musical talent. In addition to the classics, he was much adored for playing his own compositions and performed in the best concert halls across the globe. The man took great pleasure in listening to recordings of his friend's music when the mood took him.

Although his friends travelled the world, all four men made every effort to meet up once a year around Christmastime. This years' meeting was imminent and, as usual, the man felt a mixture of excitement and disquiet, reminded once more of the little he had achieved in comparison to his childhood pals.

Finally, after greeting each other with warmth and enthusiasm, they made their way to one of the finest restaurants in the city. Conversation flowed as they enjoyed fine wine and good food, and the man's three friends talked at length about their latest achievements, each revelling in success and the comfortable lifestyle it had brought. They were sparkling company for the man and he laughed out loud as jokes and anecdotes were shared by all. It was with a tinge of sadness that he turned the key in his front door when the evening was over, knowing it would be another year before they met again.

The following day brought a surprise for him however. Unbeknown to the others, each of his friends, in turn, contacted him to arrange a visit, on the understanding that it would be just the two of them.

The man was intrigued, but encouraged by the fact that each one should take time out of their busy schedule to share his company again before leaving. His dwelling was warm and comfortable, and only briefly did it cross his mind that his friends may consider his home too modest in comparison to their own.

His first visitor was the musician. As he served coffee and cake, the man noticed that his friend seemed a little subdued. He asked if something was worrying him.

It was as though the floodgates had been opened. He talked and talked about his difficulties. Because so much of his time was spent travelling, composing and preparing his pieces for the concerts, there was no room in his life for relationship. His quiet nature had compounded the issue and he was desperately lonely. His pain was obvious as he told the man of brief relationships which had failed because of work commitments and the man was filled with compassion for his friend, lending his ear to everything he had to say. By the end of the evening his friend looked much brighter. He said the man had helped him greatly, and showed much gratitude for his wise words and warm hospitality. There and then, he made the decision to perform only six times a year, leaving room in his busy life for 'fun and socialising'. The man had given him hope for a better future and one which may include someone to love.

Then came the artist. The man thought his friend seemed distracted and, after a while, asked him if he had something on his mind. Relief spread across his friend's face. He said he was surrounded by sycophants in the world of art and never knew who to trust. Always, he was struggling to discern who was genuine and this constantly undermined his well-being. Because of this, he had become less inclined to allow people close to him, isolating himself to the point that he was beginning to worry about his well-being. However, he was pleased to tell the man that spending time with old friends he knew well had made him feel so much better about himself. The man listened as his friend talked about all the things that had happened to him, and why he could no longer trust in those who surrounded his work life. He was touched by his friend's honesty and reassured him, for his emotions were fragile. In time, the man's friend looked much happier and thanked him for his encouragement. By the end of the evening, he had decided to spend more time with his old friends, whose interest in his company was genuine, and he would spend less time travelling. As the friend left, he thanked the man for giving him greater confidence in himself, and hope for a happier, more balanced future.

Finally came the professor. As soon as he walked through the door he was talking enthusiastically. Then when they finally sat down, he shared his knowledge of the man's neighbourhood, telling him how wonderfully interesting it was. In fact, the man found it impossible to squeeze a word between his friend's lively discourse for quite a while. But when he finally stopped, he turned to the man with tears in his eyes. The man comforted him as he wept and gave him the opportunity to speak freely and in complete confidence. His friend was relieved to share his secret, confessing that the wisdom he shared with so many, through his lectures and books, was lost in regard to his own life. Filled with shame, he sobbed that his life was a sham and he was no less than a charlatan who played the part of a wise man well. The man was saddened to learn that his friend had always regretted his career choice, and surprised to discover he had dreamed of becoming an actor when he was young.

Two hours and two large slices of cake later, the friend was feeling much lighter. For the first time in years, he had spoken freely and honestly. Before he left that evening, he had decided to retire early, live off the proceeds from his books, and downsize to the man's neighbourhood, where there was apparently a thriving Amateur Dramatics Society. He thanked the man for his wise words and encouragement, and gave him the longest hug before skipping down the steps to take his cab home.

By the following year the four friends were meeting every month at a modest restaurant around the corner from the man's home, after which they would take a stroll back with him to share cocoa and home-made cake. Each of his friends had talked together about how their old pal had quietly changed their lives for the better. They were forever grateful for his listening ear and kindness, and agreed that he had given them much more than they were ever able to give him in return.

~~~

Let us not measure ourselves by the lives or achievements of others.
Instead, let us make the most of who we are, and be a good friend.

Teacher
Politician…Mentor
Youth Leader…Childminder
Church Minister
Office Manager…Hospital Porter
Police Officer…Nursery Nurse
Doctor…Counsellor
Medical Consultant
Physiotherapist…GP
Nurse…Girl Guide Leader
Church Youth Leader
Paramedic…Children's Home worker
Football Trainer
Prison Officer…Home Help
Charity Worker
Volunteer…Court Judge
Professor…Care Assistant
Lecturer…Foster Parent
Nursery Leader
Sports Instructor
Shop Manager…Support Worker
Bus driver
Taxi Driver…Orphanage worker
Care Home Staff
Probation Officer
Dance Instructor…Gymnastics Instructor
Swimming Instructor…Victim Support Worker
Hotel Manager…Photographer
Scout Leader…Akela

If our desire for authority is not rooted in
integrity,
then it is *flawed*.

Well, there we are...

...my second book of poetry and tales. I hope you enjoyed reading it as much as I enjoyed writing it.

I'm happy to say that I have finally picked up my paint brushes and dipped back into the beautiful world of watercolours. So much of my poetry is focussed on nature and I don't think I'll ever stop taking nature photographs, many of which I've posted on my Facebook Author Page. Nature is a beautiful thing and so good for us to spend time with.

As you know a little more about me than you did before, it would be lovely to know more about you too, feel free to contact me and tell me what you think.

Take care.

Rona x

Please turn the page for information about other works.

Snippets of Reviews
for this and previous publications

Poetry: Another Tapestry of Words

Damsels and Dragons
"What a beautiful poem. So full of wonderful imagery. The process is pretty amazing and the author has captured the magic and mystery very descriptively." Nature Lover.
The British Dragonfly Society liked this poem so much that they shared it on their Facebook Page.

Blackbird
"The poem entitled 'Blackbird' is beautiful and I love the author's description of its song. It is such a magical sound and she expresses it so perfectly. I also like the blackbird's eye being 'starlight cloaked in ebony velvet.' Gorgeous!"
Lesley Rawlinson, Author.

Earth's Bones
"The author shows great insight into the Earth's amazing processes in the poem 'Earth's Bones'. I love it!"
Jennifer Jones, Earth Scientist and Author.

Poetry: A Tapestry of Words (My first)

"Some very emotive poems sparking memories; contemplation; some smiles and some sadness." P.A.
"Beautiful and sometimes poignant." C.B.
"I really like these poems. The author has a subtle use of language and I believe she's spiritual." ~ A.M.
"Insightful, the Author is reading my mind!" ~ S.C

Silver Key

"You will not be disappointed with this next book of The Light Keepers series! I absolutely loved it and was moved to tears in some parts and laughing out loud in others."

"Star's journey took us through magical portals, and introduced an array of new and interesting characters, including a couple on the dark side."

"I can't wait for the next book now, I loved reading about the struggle between darkness and light and the inner struggles of the characters. It so true to life!"

"An enjoyable story, with a hint of a new adventure to come."

"They are absolutely brilliant books! I couldn't put them down as I was so excited to find out what happens next. I can't wait until my daughter is old enough to read them, I know she's going to love them."

Star's Awakening

"The author has created a really vivid world. The book is easy to read and nicely paced."

"I thoroughly enjoyed it. It was one of those books I just wanted to keep on turning the pages to find out what was happening next."

"I thoroughly enjoyed this book. The characters were easy to visualise."

"A good story line and great characterisation."

"I was totally drawn into the life of the central family."

"It was amazing. I absolutely loved the story line and the characters!! Can't wait for the next book in the series."

"An interesting and enjoyable read, I was drawn into the story right from the beginning."

"I was intrigued, it was complex, I couldn't put it down."

Cont'd...

120

My novels are available n Kindle and in paperback

Two stories with just a touch of fantasy. These tales follow Star and her family through the twists and turns of family life as she becomes an adult. Old secrets are uncovered and new friends and enemies are made as their journey unfolds.

Star's Awakening and The Silver Key feature the age-old struggle between good and evil, and the family's journey through it. The tales begin in Gawswood, a close-knit community with Star's family is at the heart of it.

Star's Awakening – Lightkeepers Book One
Star's widowed father is the settle Elder. All is well, but as Star prepares for her coming of age, everything begins to change. Old enemies, the discovery of family secrets, and life-changing events lead us through their journey.

The Silver Key – Lightkeepers Book Two
The continuation of *Star's Awakening* picks up the family's tale five years later. Life in Gawswood has been good - but all is not as it seems. We watch the human condition weaving its way through the trials and tribulations that beset them. Interesting new characters join them as they search for answers and closure.

Speckled Wood Butterfly

Printed in Great Britain
by Amazon